KEYBOARD LITERATURE

Timeless Gems From the 18th, 19th & 20th Centuries

THE MUSIC TREE
PART 3

**Selected and Edited
by
Frances Clark
Louise Goss
Sam Holland**

PREFACE

Beginning with **MUSIC TREE PART 3** and its companion **ACTIVITIES PART 3,** the *Frances Clark Library for Piano Students* now includes an exciting core curriculum made up of:

> **Keyboard Literature 3**
> **Keyboard Technic 3**
> **Students' Choice 3**

The new **KEYBOARD LITERATURE** books contain a wide variety of choice small keyboard works from the 17th through 20th centuries. The pieces are by the great masters from each period who wrote music easy enough for students at that level. In addition, we have included the best pieces by "minor masters," those teacher-composers whose delightful music is ideally suited to students.

All of the selections are original keyboard works. In many of the 17th and 18th century pieces, where composers did not provide dynamics, phrasing or articulation, we have added light editing. Most of the 19th and 20th century music was carefully edited by the composer, and we have left it untouched except for suggested fingering. The goal of each volume is to provide a well-rounded and nourishing diet of musical periods, forms, types and styles in pieces that have sure-fire student appeal.

The technical skills for each volume are prepared for in the corresponding **KEYBOARD TECHNIC** book. The theoretical concepts and skills needed at each level are supported by the corresponding **MUSIC TREE ACTIVITIES** book. For each level there is a **STUDENTS' CHOICE**, made up of recreational music for pure fun.

We express deep gratitude to faculty of the Preparatory Departments at The New School for Music Study, Southern Methodist University, Concordia University and Louisiana State University who have tested pilot editions. In addition, we thank colleagues across the country who have participated in surveys, questionnaires and test-teaching, and whose feedback has greatly facilitated our work in preparing these new editions.

We hope you will enjoy teaching this series as much as we have, and that your students will share with ours the joy and excitement of this great repertoire.

CONTENTS

In music, the time from 1750 until the early 1800s is known as the Classical Period. It was a time of great historical events, including both the French and American Revolutions. Famous people who lived during this period include George Washington, Benjamin Franklin, Napoleon Bonaparte and the author, Jane Austen.

Music composed during the Classical period is usually graceful and elegant. Keyboard pieces include dances such as the minuet and gigue. The piano (invented in 1709) became very popular as great composers, including Haydn, Mozart and Beethoven, created works that are still loved throughout the world today. You will study their music in *Keyboard Literature, Book 4*.

James Hook (1746-1827)
Born in England, Hook was organist and composer at the famous Marylbone Gardens in London. He was also an excellent teacher, and his piano instruction book, *Guide to Music*, was widely used by English piano students.

Alexander Reinagle (1756-1809)
Reinagle was an English-born pianist, teacher and composer who spent most of his professional life in the United States. He was director of a Philadelphia theater company for which he wrote an opera called "Columbus," about the discovery of America. He is said to have introduced four-hand piano music to this country, and to have composed the first piano sonatas written here.

Daniel Gottlob Türk (1756-1813)
Born in the same year as Mozart, Türk was a German pianist, composer and teacher. His first teacher was his father and later he took lessons from a student of J.S. Bach. Türk was an excellent teacher who wrote a great deal of music for his piano students.

Anton Diabelli (1781-1858)
Despite his Italian name, Diabelli was an Austrian composer. He was a friend of Franz Joseph Haydn and studied with Haydn's brother, Michael. Diabelli was a popular teacher of piano and guitar. Later he started his own publishing firm and was often the first to publish the compositions of Beethoven and Schubert.

Samuel Arnold (1740-1802)
Arnold was an English organist and composer who is remembered primarily for an edition he made of Handel's music. The *Gigue* comes from a set of lessons he wrote for his harpsichord students.

Minuetto

from Guide to Music

James Hook
(1746-1827)

With dignity

Allegro in C

Alexander Reinagle
(1756-1809)

Gracefully

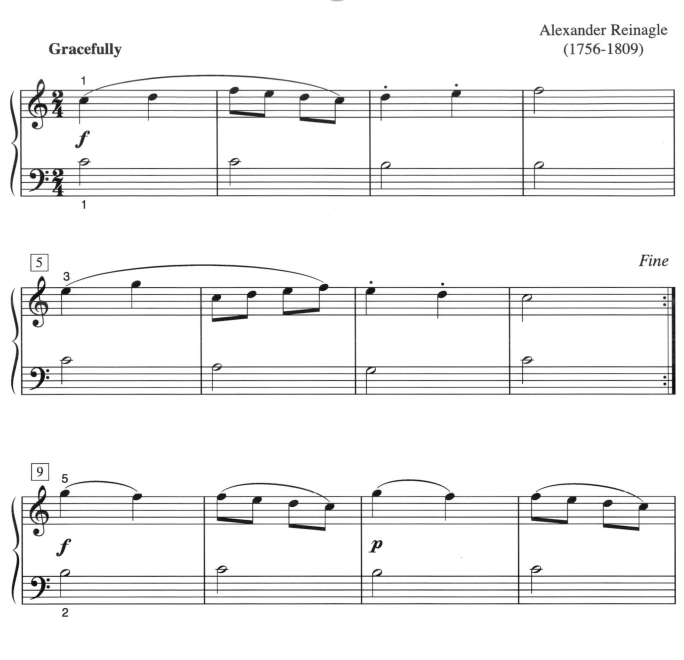

Fine

D.C. al Fine

Minuetto

Alexander Reinagle
(1756-1809)

Brightly but not hurried

Frolic

From 60 Pieces for Aspiring Players, Vol. 1

Daniel Gottlob Türk
(1756-1813)

Carefree

From 60 Pieces for Aspiring Players, Vol. 1

Daniel Gottlob Türk
(1756-1813)

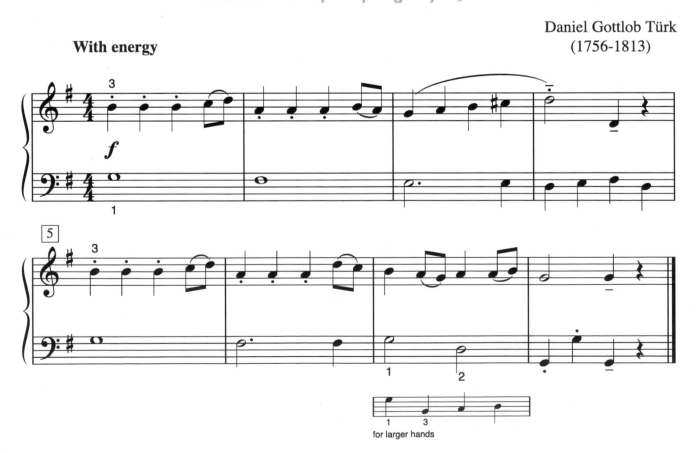

for larger hands

Melody

Anton Diabelli
(1781-1858)

Singing

Bagatelle

Anton Diabelli
(1781-1858)

With Motion

Gigue

From *Lessons for Harpsichord*

Samuel Arnold
(1740-1802)

With a lilt

The Romantic Period in music spans the years from the early 1800s to about 1900. In America, this was a time of westward expansion, the California Gold Rush and the development of the railroad and the steam engine. It was also the time of the American Civil War and the end of slavery. Among many great historical figures are Abraham Lincoln, Florence Nightingale, Alexander Graham Bell and the English author, Charles Dickens.

The greatest Romantic piano composers included Schubert, Chopin, Schumann and Brahms. It was a century of great virtuoso pianists and much of the finest and best-loved piano music comes from this period. The focus of the Western cultural world was still on Europe, but America was beginning to produce its own performers and composers.

The music is called "romantic" because it is filled with long melodic lines, rich harmonies and intense emotions. Composers often wrote short musical pictures called "character pieces" with descriptive titles but they also developed much longer works with titles such as "prelude", "intermezzo" and "ballade".

Ferdinand Beyer (1803-1863)

Beyer was a popular German piano teacher and composer. In 1850, he wrote a piano method, *Beginning Studies for Piano*, that is still in world-wide use today.

Kaspar Jacob Bischoff (1823-1893)

Bischoff was a well-known German composer, theorist and teacher who founded a sacred choral society in Frankfurt. His compositions include symphonies, overtures, chamber music and piano compositions as well as a *Manual of Harmony*.

Cornelius Gurlitt (1820-1901)

Gurlitt's long life spanned the entire Romantic era. Born in Germany, he was trained as a pianist and organist. As a young man, he spent five years studying composition in Denmark. He enjoyed friendships with many of the great composers of his time, such as Schumann and Brahms. He wrote hundreds of pieces for his piano students, including those in this collection.

Wilhelm M. Vogel (1846-1922)

Like so many other German composers of his day, Vogel was a well-known piano teacher. He composed a large 12-part piano method for his own students that was widely used throughout Germany by other teachers. "Brave Knight" comes from this method.

Thoughtful and Playful

From Op. 101

Ferdinand Beyer
(1803-1863)

Morning Greeting

Kasper Jacob Bischoff
(1823-1893)

Little Dance

From *A Collection of the Most Beautiful Pieces for Beginners*

Cornelius Gurlitt
(1820-1901)

Gracefully

Song

Cornelius Gurlitt
(1820-1901)

Flowing smoothly

Brave Knight

Wilheim M. Vogel
(1846-1922)

Robustly

The 20th Century was an era of science, technology and experimentation. Inventions such as radio, television, computers, the Internet, manned flight and space travel brought people from around the world into closer contact. But it was also a period of two devastating world wars. Among the great figures of the time were Albert Einstein, Mahatma Ghandi, Franklin Roosevelt and Winston Churchill.

Music written in the 20th century is also filled with experimentation. Composers such as Debussy, Stravinsky, Bartok and our own American, Aaron Copland, used every form and technique from the Classical and Romantic periods, but also invented new ones—new scales, colorful and dissonant harmonies and wild, exciting rhythms.

Vladimir Rebikov (1866-1920)

Rebikov was an outstanding Russian composer of the early 20th century. When he first started composing, he liked to imitate Tchaikovsky, but later, he developed his own composing style. "The Bear"is from one of his many piano works, *The Christmas Gift*.

Béla Bartók (1881-1945)

Bartok was a Hungarian virtuoso pianist and one of the greatest composers of the 20th century. He collected peasant folk songs and dances and used them in his music. Our two pieces are from *First Term at the Piano*, part of his piano method.

Alexandre Tansman (1897-1986)

Tansman was born in Poland but spent most of his life in Paris. During the Second World War, he lived in the United States. He was a pianist, conductor and composer whose music is filled with beautiful melodies and energetic rhythms. This "Folk Dance" was written especially for the *Frances Clark Library*.

Ernst Bacon (1898-1990)

Bacon was an American pianist, conductor and composer. He was assistant conductor of the Rochester (NY) Opera Company and taught piano at the Eastman School of Music. He wrote many symphonies and choral works, and a charming collection for children, *It's A Kid's World*, from which "Doodlebug" is taken.

Alexander Tcherepnin (1899-1977)

Tcherepnin grew up in a famous musical household. His father, Nicolai, was one of the most important Russian composers. Alexander first studied with his father and later at the St. Petersburg Conservatory. While still in his teens, he was considered one of the most promising pianists and composers in the country. He completed his musical studies in Paris, traveled around the world, and finally settled in the United States. He wrote these pieces especially for the *Frances Clark Library*.

Norman Dello-Joio (b. 1913)

Dello-Joio is an American composer of Italian descent. He studied piano and organ at home with his father and by the time he was 12, would occasionally substitute for his father as a church organist. As a young man, he toured with his own jazz band. Later, he was musical director of a ballet company and taught composition at Sara Lawrence College. He has written many fine piano works such as "Mountain Melody" from *Suite for the Young*.

John LaMontaine (b. 1921)

LaMontaine is an American composer and pianist who studied at the Eastman School of Music, Chicago Musical College, the Julliard School and the American Conservatory in Fontainebleau, France. For four years, he was the NBC Symphony pianist under the great conductor, Arturo Toscanini. In 1959, his First Piano Concerto won the Pulitzer prize for music. He wrote all of the music in the Music Workbooks of the *Frances Clark Library*. One of the most beautiful of these pieces is "Moon Mist".

David Kraehenbuehl (1923-1997)

Kraehenbuehl was an American composer born in Illinois. By the time he was ten, he had already written many short piano pieces. As he was growing up, he couldn't decide whether to become a mathematician or musician, so he studied both subjects all his life. He taught music theory and composition at Colorado College, Yale University and the New School for Music Study. "March of the Trolls" and "Daydreaming" are two of the many pieces he wrote for the *Frances Clark Library*.

Dianne Goolkasian-Rahbee (b. 1938)

Goolkasian Rahbee is a first-generation Armenian-American who has become one of the prominent women composers of our time. She was born in Massachusetts and had her musical training in Boston, New York and Salzburg, Austria. She is a fine concert pianist who also concentrates on composing and on supporting the work of other women composers. She has written pieces for piano solo, orchestra, instrumental ensembles, percussion and voice. Her collection of student pieces, *Pictures*, includes "Snowflakes Gently Falling".

Nancy Telfer (b. 1939)

Telfer is a leading Canadian composer who has composed over 200 works for different instruments. She was born in Ontario, and studied at the University of Western Ontario. Her music is marked by vital rhythms, unusual harmonies and witty surprises. "Dance of the Elephant" is from her first collection of piano solos, *Put on Your Dancing Shoes*.

The Bear

From The Christmas Gifts, No. 4

Vladimir Rebikov
(1866-1920)

Awkward and lumbering

Folk Song

From *First Term at the Piano*

Béla Bartók
(1881-1945)

Moderately

Dialogue

From *First Term at the Piano*

Béla Bartók
(1881-1945)

Moderately

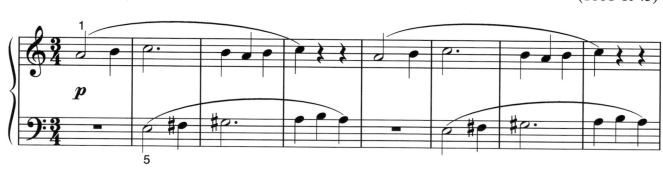

Folk Dance

From *Contemporary Piano Literature, Book I*

Alexandre Tansman
(1897-1986)

Fast and bright

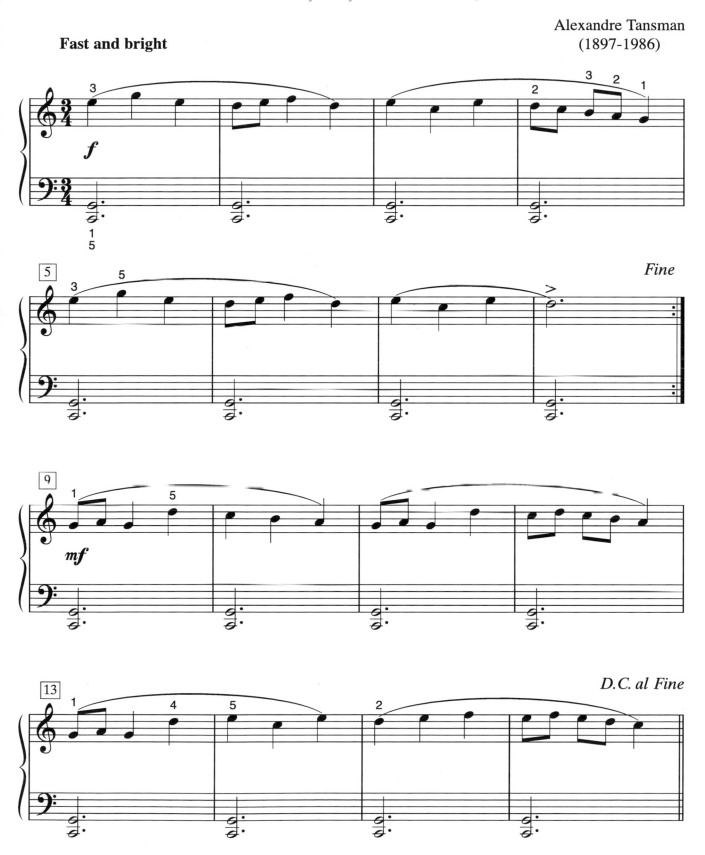

Doodlebug

From *It's a Kid's World*

Ernst Bacon
(1898-1990)

March

From *Contemporary Piano Literature, Book I*

Alexander Tcherepnin
(1899-1977)

In march time

Joy and Tears

From Contemporary Piano Literature, Book I

Alexander Tcherepnin
(1899-1977)

Rather fast

Mountain Melody

From *Suite for the Young*

Norman Dello-Joio
(b. 1913)

With simplicity

Moon Mist

From *Music Workbook 1B, The Frances Clark Library*

John LaMontaine
(b. 1920)

Dreamily, but with motion

March of the Trolls

From *Contemporary Piano Literature, Book I*

David Kraehenbuehl
(1923-1997)

Daydreaming

From *Contemporary Piano Literature, Book I*

David Kraehenbuehl
(1923-1997)

Snowflakes Gently Falling

From Pictures, Op. 3

Dianne Goolkasian-Rahbee
(1938-   )

Tenderly

with two pedals throughout

in place

Ballet at Dusk

From *Put on Your Dancing Shoes*

Nancy Telfer
(1939-   )

Dance of the Elephant

From Put on Your Dancing Shoes

Nancy Telfer
(1939-   )

Clumsily and not fast

accent (>). A sudden emphasis on a tone to make it stand out from others.

acciacatura ( ). An ornament played just before or together with the main note of a melody, and released immediately.

accompaniment. Musical background for a melody.

bagatelle. A short character piece, often for piano.

ballet. A performance by dancers to music, usually in costumes and with scenery.

bitonal. Using two different keys at the same time.

chamber music. Instrumental music written for a small group, a performer to each part.

character piece. A composition that conveys a mood or paints a picture.

choral. Music written for a choir.

composer. A musician who writes music.

conductor. A musician who directs a group of performers.

crescendo ( ). Gradually louder.

dance. Moving rhythmically to music.

Da Capo al fine (D. C. al fine). Repeat the piece from the beginning and end at the place marked "fine".

decrescendo ( ). Gradually softer.

dialogue. A composition that sounds like two people having a conversation.

drone. An accompaniment of long repeated notes, usually in the lowest part.

dynamic marks (*pp, p, mp, mf, f, ff*). Signs that show the performer how loud or soft to play.

edition. A collection of a composer's works.

folk dance. Traditional dance from a culture.

forte (*f*). Loud.

fortissimo (*ff*). Very loud.

gigue. A lively dance that often has the rhythmic pattern of ♩ ♪ ♩ ♪ .

harmony. Several tones sounding together.

harpsichord. The most popular keyboard instrument in the 16th and 17th centuries. Its tone is produced by tiny picks plucking the strings.

jazz. A style of music that began in the southern United States at the end of the 19th century. Jazz uses African rhythms, European harmonies and American gospel music.

legato. Smoothly.

march. Music with a steady rhythm, suitable for a group of people marching together.

melody. A successive group of pitches that belong together in a way that has shape, to be sung by the voice or played by an instrument.

mezzo forte (*mf*). Medium loud.

mezzo piano (*mp*). Medium soft.

minuet. A graceful dance in 3/4 time.

minuetto. A term used by many composers for their shorter minuets.

non legato. Not smoothly.

octave. The distance from one note to the next note that has the same name, for example, from one C to the next C.

octave higher (*8va------*). Play the note an octave higher than it is written.

octave lower (*8va------*). Play the note an octave lower than it is written.

opera. A drama that is set to music to be sung on stage accompanied by an orchestra.

opus (op.). Work. Used by composers to show in what order a work was written.

organ. A keyboard instrument that produces sound when air is blown through pipes, controlled by a performer's use of the keyboard and pedals.

ornaments. Notes that decorate a melody.

ostinato. A musical or rhythmic figure that is repeated throughout a piece.

overture. An instrumental piece that introduces an opera or other major works.

pedal. A part of keyboard instruments that is controlled by the feet.

perfect fifth. The distance between the first and the fifth scale degrees of a scale.

piano. A keyboard instrument that produces sounds when hammers, controlled by the keys, hit the strings.

piano (*p*). Soft.

pianissimo (*pp*). Very soft.

repeat sign ( ). Go back to the beginning of the section or to this sign and play the section again.

rhythm. How time is organized in music.

scale. A group of notes arranged in a specific order of rising pitches.

sforzando (*sfz*). A sudden loud accent.

slur ( ). Notes within this sign belong together and should be played as smoothly as possible.

sonata. A composition, usually with several movements, written for piano or piano with another instrument.

song. A composition that has words, and is to be sung.

staccato ( ). Short and detached.

symphony. A composition for orchestra that usually has several movements.

tenuto ( ). Hold the note to its full value.

virtuoso. A performer or performance that shows high technical and artistic abilities.

whole-tone scale. A scale in which the notes are a whole step away from one another.